AF084363

THE FASHION BRAND GUIDE TO

Holiday Sales Planning at any Time of the Year

GETTING A HEAD START IN
Q1/Q2 & LAST MINUTE
Q3/Q4 STRATEGIES

BY SYAMA MEAGHER

© 2015 Syama Meagher, All rights reserved.

ISBN: 978-1-329-57582-0

ABOUT SCALING RETAIL:

Scaling Retail is a boutique retail-consulting firm that focuses on the development of retail properties and fashion brands. Helmed by Syama Meagher, CEO, and retail expert with 15 years of retail experience she brings a wealth of information in retail planning and merchandising. With offices out of Los Angeles and New York, we work with international and domestic brands in developing innovative growth strategies. Often called upon as a hired consultant to bring retail experience to the table, we can offer comprehensive project management, leadership and oversight to ensure successful project completion.

ABOUT SYAMA MEAGHER:

Syama is the co-author of the Fashion Designers Guide to Creating Fashion Websites that Sell. She has been interviewed for Refinery 29, United States National Public Radio (NPR), Glammonitor, Daily Worth, U.S. News & World Report, and most recently profiled as an inspiring female entrepreneur on Lady Guns Global. She has previously dedicated her expertise working for Gucci, Barney's New York, Macy's and AHAlife and brings relevant insight on various topics such as retail consulting and retail market strategies. Previous speaking engagements include, American Express CEO Boot camp, Fashion Business Inc. The Pool Tradeshow, and StartUp Fashion.

Follow @ScalingRetail on Instagram, Twitter, Facebook, YouTube & LinkedIn for news and events.

HELLO THERE,

Welcome! You are one step closer to launching an excellent holiday sales campaign. I'm excited to share with you this guide that has been compiled from years of working with fashion brands on exactly this topic. This is an important topic that can often get overlooked during the year and rushed at the end. Topics like *Assortment Planning, Markdowns, Pricing, Digital and Direct Marketing* are covered in this guide. Whether you are in the middle of Fall or just starting off the New Year, this guide will be a handy resource for you.

Did you know? The holiday season is your opportunity to make 60% of your yearly sales in 3 months. If you are a new brand, you may not be taking advantage of future planning. I understand, it can be tough, especially if you are working your business strategy on a month-to-month basis. I cannot stress enough how future planning will help you and your business. Not only to decrease your stress, but to build the right relationships to execute an effective strategy.

In this strategy guide I break down the process into 2 phases: Getting a Head Start: Holiday Sales Planning in Q1/Q2 and Last Minute Planning: Holiday Sales Planning in Q3/Q4.

Send me an email (syama@scalingretail.com) and let me know how this works for you.

To your success!
Syama

CEO, Scaling Retail
www.ScalingRetail.com

PART ONE

Getting a Head Start:
HOLIDAY PLANNING IN Q1/Q2

Great news, you are getting a head start on planning for the holiday season. This will allow you to make better choices, and ultimately make more sales. Did you know that many brands wait until the weeks before the holiday season starts to come up with a plan? This generally can lead to haste decision making, poor allocation of financial resources ultimately not allowing you to make the best choices for your business. If you are in the Last Minute camp, don't fret, you can continue to read on, but feel free to skip ahead to the Last Minute Planning chapter to get a strategy you can implement today.

PRODUCTS

Assortment Planning:

Increasing retail demands coupled with the traditional Increasing retail demands coupled with the traditional manufacturing processes can make it a little challenging to compete with big brands that can deliver new styles each month. Often times manufactures will put your needs last since they have larger brands to fulfill. This should be taken into consideration when line planning. If you are planning F/W 2020 to show in February 2020 it's a good idea to start to plan out what styles will be August/September deliveries and what will be arriving in October or even Resort (November/December). Have that discussion with your manufacturers and know what those minimums and costs are. Keep the assortment tight with the knowledge that you may end up marking them down relatively quickly. Timing is important if you decide to do brand collaborations or even introduce new exclusives.

Markdowns and Pricing:

Since holiday selling is not only the best time of year to generate revenue but also notorious for sales and markdowns it's important to build additional margins into your wholesale or retail price point. If you have the opportunity to sell something special for holiday that is less expensive to produce than the Fall collection but can be priced competitively, you are in luck. POS Sales (point of sale, short term sales) generally start Thanksgiving. Those tend to be at 25%-40% off. These sales typically last 3 days and prices go back up to full price after. At the same time, you may be running a coupon code for your newsletter 15% off (don't allow people to double dip - only one coupon at a time). December you may run another POS Sale running until Christmas, followed by a hard markdown December 26th. The main difference between a hard markdown and POS Sale is that a markdown is permanent- once you mark it down 50% off it stays there- therefor you will want to use it sparingly. All of this talk about markdowns and POS is to get you prepped on pricing. If you currently only have a 2x markup on your products- you may not be able to take advantage of these sale opportunities. If you are a luxury brand, and sales are not a part of your strategy, you will want to consider other incentives that equate to dollar values such as: Gift With Purchase (GWP), customization or limited edition product exclusives. Either way, the holiday has financial implications that need to be considered when pricing the collection.

MARKETING

Your marketing strategy will be a combination of paid and unpaid activities. While you might be thinking that you will only be doing unpaid activities its important keep in mind that there might still be some costs associated with it. Creating graphic assets for your Instagram and making sure supporting graphics are on your website with a pop up or banner might require some help from your developer and graphic designer. If you layer in the paid activities you will want to make sure they are supported by unpaid media and associated graphic assets. So as you go through the different ideas proposed, please don't just rely on one. A proper campaign has supporting assets across channels. In addition, its important not to take on everything that one could possibly do. As a small company, being picky is oh so important. At the end of the day move on your unpaid media strategies and pick a couple paid direct and digital opportunities.

Step 1: Research

Digital Marketing:

This is a great time to start to research the channels you want to have a presence on. Who is going to be spreading your brand message and what are the outlets. As you research your competitors and what they did just a few months prior (pretty easy to see on social) keep in mind that you may have a different budget or bandwidth then they do, so picking channels carefully will be integral for your investment. Combine your research with the channels that are currently working for you. These channels should include: social media, dedicated blog posts, dedicated newsletters, giveaways (podcasts, newsletters), Instagram/YouTube/Pinterest influencers, SEO and SEM. Don't forget to include your own website/ecommerce platform (traffic, analytics). After all, this is where you will be including banner ads, light box popups and driving sales.

Social Media:

Are you on all the social platforms? Are you doing it well? Evaluate your channels and time invested. Platforms like Instagram, Pinterest and Facebook should grace your top 3. Channels like YouTube and Twitter need a special focus. If you don't have the time to do it well, don't do it. You can monitor your competition all year long, so take close note when and what they are doing for paid media.

For a more in depth look on suggested channels and budgets, check out the Last Minute Planning Section.

Cost to Create: $0-$100, this depends on if you are generating your own graphic assets and how much your budget is for advertising. I always suggest starting off with $50 over 5 days to test.
Time Needed to Setup: Less than a week- or as soon as you can get assets created. Don't forget to support your digital marketing ad with assets on your website.

Dedicated Blog Posts:

Bloggers aren't cheap. They have spent time and money investing in their platforms and rely on advertisers (you), to help recoup their investment. They provide you with instant access to a core demographic and have a trusted word. While it may sound like a match made in heaven, most consumers can tell and know if a post is paid. Nowadays bloggers will be very choosy about who they work with so as to prevent looking like they 'sold out' or are diluted by sponsors. Its important when researching potential bloggers for paid advertising that you understand exactly what you are getting.

Questions to Ask: How many readers do you have? How much traffic does your site get? What's the conversion rate that you get with brands like mine? Will this be the only post of the day? Will you promote it on your other social media platforms? Will you feature the brand/product or is it part of a collection? What do you need from me? If I'm sending you a product, will I get it back? And of course, How much?

Cost to Create: $500- $5,000.
Time Needed to Setup: Smaller bloggers less time, bigger bloggers think 6 months out.

Dedicated Newsletters:

Just like paid blog posts, dedicated newsletters are often easy to spot due to the 'dedicated' header in the email subject line. These are best reserved for announcing live events or online promotions. As a small brand I would suggest using dedicated newsletters in a partnership capacity with other brands that are showing at an event or if you are selling online at a store and want to go into co-op advertising (where you share in the cost of the advertising). You will need to budget for the creation of the graphics, copywriting and the ad placement itself.

Cost to Create: $500 and up depending on the reach of the online newsletter.
Time Needed to Setup: Between 2-6 months.

Banner Ads:

Traditional banner ads are a great way to announce sales. Oftentimes cheaper than the dedicated newsletter route, banner ads are easy to re-market and very effective. As you research your preferred outlets for your digital marketing strategy keep the banner ad in mind. Most channels will include varying sizes and prices on the rate card and list the traffic and expected conversion. Find out the length of time your anticipated banner ad will be up and ask if you can swap it out with other options if its not performing as anticipated. This will require that you have multiple advertisements mocked up, but you will be happy you did. Expect to spend money on your graphic assets and the ad placement.

Cost to Create: $50-$2,000
Time Needed to Setup: Depending on how large the outlet is you will want to give yourself between 2-6 months.

Social Media Giveaways:

Who doesn't love something free? Drive likes, shares, and followers through strategic giveaways on social and through other outlets. This is a great way to get your brand in front of blogger and influencer outlets. Maybe you can put together a few items that were slow sellers during the year or even create a couple exclusives that you can photograph and bundle together for giveaways. This will of course cost you some money, but could be a great incentive to activate new and existing customers. Use the giveaway as an opportunity to reach out to potential collaborators as well. Maybe a brand in a different product category but also targeting the same demographic would be interested in cross marketing with a joint giveaway. Take this as an opportunity to get creative and remember that once you launch a giveaway you need to create the supporting graphic assets and keep it alive for a set period of time.

Cost to Create: depends on the price of your product and if you are targeting/collaborating with an influencer
Time Needed to Setup: 3 months

Influencers:

The new Digital Influencers are on Instagram, Pinterest, Twitter, and of course bloggers. There are also niche influencers on sites like Poshmark (peer to peer), Keep (affiliate marketing), and other sites where people aggregate to shop. Look into these sites as places where you tap into the high-ranking followers and approach them to curate your products on their feeds. For the more traditional routes (Instagram, Pinterest and Twitter) I do suggest, especially if you are on a budget, to take a look at up and coming influencers with 25,000 + followers.

Do your due diligence before signing on any influencer. This means looking at follower numbers, engagement numbers, ask about their conversion for paid posts, find out how long your post gets to be featured and take a look at who their followers are. Just because an influencer has a lot of followers, doesn't mean that they are the right target for you. Find out who creates the posts and assets and make sure your influencer has what they need to do the best job for you.

Cost to Create: $0- $2,000
Time Needed to Setup: 1-3 months.

SEO:

Never under estimate the power of Search Engine Optimization. This should really be part of a long-term strategy for your brand. SEO comes from on page and off page strategies. On page, make sure your product copy is strong, all images have proper titles, and on your backend you have all the title pages and meta descriptions in place. If you have a blog, keep it updated. Off page it's important to take your content and ensure it gets syndicated across all channels appropriate to your brand.

This can take some time and oftentimes brands will hire SEO experts to manage this side of the business since it is a tough slog to index and share. If you are keeping a consistent blog try staggering out the release of your content across channels so as to keep content fresh. SEO over time will help you in ranking on search.

Keep in mind though; this is a process that takes time. If you start working on it now it could take years to see real improvements on search unless you have the budget or a very niche product.

Cost to Create: $0-$150/month. Depending if you outsource or not.
Time Needed to Setup: ongoing strategy.

SEM:

To generate a good amount of traffic from Search Engine Marketing, at least enough traffic to make it worthwhile, I suggest creating a set of experiments to test and see what target words attract the highest converting ads. I would do this early on in the year so that when the holiday season comes around you know what target words and phrases to include in your SEM. While you can do SEM on all search engines, the one I would suggest would be Google. As a small business there are SEM coupons that companies like Google will provide you, so sign up for an Adwords account and sit tight while they send you one.

Cost to Create: your tests can run between $100-$200, and when holiday comes around beef it up to $200-$300/month.
Time Needed to Setup: 2-3 hours.

Remember to Look to Niche Markets:

Most brands will look to larger media platforms to get the word out, think Refinery29, The Cut, and Fashionista. These are great platforms, and if you plan your budget and supporting media assets accordingly can be extremely profitable. But don't underestimate the power of smaller influencers who garner high conversions. These are bloggers, Instagram influencers, and high worth Pinterest Pinners, who have an audience and who may be less expensive to mobilize than traditional media outlets. As you research include these guys on your list.

Direct Marketing:

All good media campaigns should have a direct and digital component. Start researching the direct marketing initiatives that your competitors engaged with over the holiday season prior. These will Include: Popup Shops, Shop in Shops, Post Card Mailers, Catalogs, Flea Markets, Trunk Shows, Brand Collaborations and Holiday Events.

Popup Shops:

This is a great way to test pricing, get in front of new customers and activate existing customers. It doesn't need to be pricey to set up shop for a weekend or a month, depending on your location and if you are sharing the space. Wholesale and retail brands can both benefit from this activity. If you plan to do this activity make sure to project the following costs: Employees, Shopping Bags/Gift-wrap, Inventory, Postcards, Hangers, Rolling Racks, Digital Marketing Promo to Drive Traffic.

Cost to Create: varies between $300- $5,000
Time Needed to Setup: 1-3 months. My favorite site to search for Popup Shops is The Storefront (www.thestorefront.com).

Shop in Shops:

This strategy requires you to develop a relationship with an existing retailer. The benefits are clear- you can take advantage of existing store traffic and advertising/marketing. The retailer will have the infrastructure and you are simply showing up with inventory and some branded materials. There can be a costly element to this if you are leasing the space within a retailer; you may pay a high dollar/square foot for the space. How to do it? I suggest contacting the local store managers of retailers you want to work with. They will put you in touch with their Regional Director of Stores.

Cost to Create: varies between $2,000- $10,000
Time Needed to Setup: 6 months.

Postcards:

An easy and great way to get potential and current customers to come to your website. Postcards can be used for bounce back campaigns- add a discount to the postcard and send out with purchases, adding to event gift bags, leaving in local coffee shops, using as your business card when talking about your brand and as announcements to send out to editors, bloggers, stylists and potential buyers. Budget for Graphic Designer and potential Copywriter.

Cost to Create: $50-$150.
Time Needed to Setup: 1 week or less.

Catalogs:

This has made a comeback in recent years. Retailers and brands are coming full circle with catalogs and short magazines. Coming in all forms, the best kind of catalog is beautiful, visual and will stick around on someone's coffee table for a while. My favorite catalogs look more like editorial magazines, and are short and sweet. Get creative and think beyond just selling your product, you are selling you brand. Use this catalog similar to the post cards, but due to the costly nature of it, you may want to be a little more selective on who you send it to. You will want to budget for: Copywriter, Potential Photo-shoot, Stylist, and Graphic Designer.

Cost to Create: Big spread here: $500-$5,000.
Time Needed to Setup: 3 months.

Flea Markets:

Flea markets are an easy way to get in front of customers in an aggregated environment. Leverage your created postcards, catalogs and existing email database to get an active audience at the next flea market you show at.

How to pick the best one? Take a look at the brands that are showing at the various markets in your area. Are the price points comparable to yours? Are the brands marketing to the same target you have? Just showing at a market won't guarantee sales, so you will want to do your homework in advance to pick the right one.

Once you find the right one keep in mind you will need to fill out an application and get approved. Make sure to find out what is included in this setup: will you need to provide your own folding table and chair? Mirror? Get the hidden costs out of the way. If this turns out to be the right market, you may want to invest in signage, paid digital marketing, and packaging (shopping bags, stickers etc.).

Cost to Create: $500 approx.
Time Needed to Setup: 1-2 months.

Trunk Shows:

This is a wonderful way to test market products in retailers that you would like to build a relationship with, as well as test market pricing and styles. Its a short term activity, usually taking place over one evening or a weekend and so you really want to focus on driving traffic and showing that retailer your products are worth carrying.

How to prep? Make a list of target stores you want to work with. Start approaching the owners and store managers to find out what their process is. Give yourself time. Mostly because not all retailers will be so keen to say yes if they haven't done this before or if they don't know your brand. Think of it as relationship building. If you have the budget I'd consider having wine available, snacks, branded postcards, catalogs.

Tip: Give customers a discount if they sign up and follow you on Instagram at the event!

Cost to Create: Can be flex here: $100-$500.
Time Needed to Setup: 2-3 months to ensure you get people there.

Holiday Events:

Showing your products at holiday events can be both fun and profitable. People love to shop when sipping on cocktails, and event organizers are always looking for another reason to get more people to come to their events. This is where you come in. Be a sleuth and see what types of holiday events took place the year before. I'd suggest looking at hotels in your area and potentially reaching out to their event organizers to see whom you should get in touch with. Charities will oftentimes hold holiday fundraisers and local city governments will sponsor events too. Depending on the type of event and who the sponsors are you may need to provide: rolling racks, folding table, own POS station, mirrors, shopping bags etc. Don't forget you bounce back postcards and to publish the event on your website and all social media channels.

Tip: Have a Shopify ecommerce platform? Integrate seamlessly with their POS software to sell easily from one inventory source.

Cost to Create: $100-$4700.
Time Needed to Setup: 1-3 months.

Brand Collaborations:

Everyone loves good brand collaborations, but this activity takes some time to plan. To do it properly, I suggest planning out your collaboration when developing your FW assortment. This does mean that for a collection that will sell in October you may be in conversations with your brand collaborator some 12 months in advance. Depending on your modes of selling: ecommerce or wholesale and the size of your brand and the collaborators brand you may have some flexibility around this.

How to choose a brand collaborator? Choose someone who is marketing to your same target demographic but not in your same category sector- for example you make clothing, they make accessories. Maybe you take a signature print and add it to one of their accessories. Budget considerations: splitting the cost of samples, marketing, and inventory.

Cost to Create: Depending on your product, I'd say plan for $500 and up.
Time Needed to Setup: between 6-12 months.

Print Advertising: Magazines, Newspapers, and Periodicals:

With so much focus on digital outreach and in person events it's also valid to take a look at the traditional print advertising outlets. Magazines and newspapers have their value, especially niche publications that are geared to your target market. Now I am not suggesting that you save up your dollars for a NY Times newspaper ad, but if you are targeting college students I might suggest taking a small ad out in a college newspaper that you know will have very high targeted readership. Like with all of these campaigns it's not about just focusing on one outlet, you need to support it with digital efforts as well. Zines and small niche magazines might also be a good fit for your ad dollars. If it's the right outlet, but it's not sexy, it's ok. This isn't about a feature in Vogue; it's about making money. With this type of print media ensure the circulation is targeted to your demographic, find out all details on specs of the graphics you have to create.

Cost to Create: depending on the outlet anywhere between $150-$10,000

Time Needed to Setup: These are long lead publications which means anywhere from 1-3 months.

Step 2: Outreach

Most media outlets will start taking ad buys for holiday a few months (3-6 months) in advance. These are the most coveted spots in advertising. Often times, the prices quoted are higher then off-season advertising (Jan-Sept). As you start to outreach make sure you are getting ad rates for October/November/December. For larger media outlets you will be able to find ad rates available online, but for others a personalized email will behoove you to get this information.

What you need in order to make an informed decision: Number of followers/readers/mailing list, any information on conversion (how many people actually went to the brands site), different kinds sizes of advertisement slots available (banner ads, sidebar advertising vs. newsletter) and prices for said slots. How long will the advertisement run, and will they re-market the ad to people who do not open it (specifically for newsletters). Also ensure to ask if there are any special deals for SMB's (Small to Medium Sized Businesses).

Here is an Example Email:

Dear Julia,

I hope you are great. I'd like to inquire on your ad rates for direct and digital advertising in Q4. Could you please let me know your deadlines for submission and if you have any specials for SMB's?

Thanks!
Syama

Step 3: Develop Budget

Planning a budget is so important. I talk about this often and advise that one has a budget for at least 12-18 months out. Now, this doesn't mean that the budget doesn't change, but you have to start somewhere. Once you have gathered pricing information in the outreach process, put together an excel spreadsheet with the pricing and the outlets outreach numbers, and then start to edit. You should end up with a budget that includes your costs for a graphic designer, any web developer costs, as well as any paid media placements you are considering.

Step 4: Develop Timeline

Lets think logically about this and work backwards from a launch date in October. This example works with long lead publications like print. Short lead publications can vary depending on how big the outlet is and how far in advance they plan. As always-the more time you give yourself the better!

April: Create & Edit List of Potential Paid Media
May: Outreach to Paid Media

June: Finalize Top Choices of Paid Media
July: Confirm Paid Media Placements
August: Develop Graphic Design and Copywriting for assets
September: Finalize and submit Graphic Assets
October: Media Placement launches
November: Campaigns Continue
December: Campaigns Continue
January: Post-Mortem: Holiday Recap

Step 5: Develop Assets

As you develop assets for your marketing channels keep in mind you will to create messaging that is echoed on you website as well. If you have a special target advertising promo make sure you land that add on your shop page. If you can support it with a landing page targeted to that customer- even better. Before you have a conversation with your graphic designer make sure you know exactly what you are looking for; create a list with dimension so that your designer can check them off when completed.

Step 6: Launch

After you double check your graphic assets for visual and grammar edits, create a schedule and make sure you have supporting visuals ready for your site its time to close your eyes and press go! Hopefully your launch includes a well-rounded targeted approach that includes digital, print, a live opportunity to experience your product with a collaboration thrown in the middle. Sounds like a lot to pack into a 3 month time period, but it will create an amazing impact on your sales, traffic to your website and brand presence.

Step 7: Monitor & Pivot

To properly monitor your campaigns you will want to set up Google Analytics and make sure to familiarize yourself with the Acquisition section. This is where you will track where your click thru's are coming from. Sometimes print media can be challenging to track, but if you are offering any type of discount for the holiday, gift with purchase or other offer consider including it on your print media and create a unique code so that you can track the bounce backs.

Depending on the length of your ad placement you may have little to no time to react to the engagement on your ad. If you have time on your campaigns monitor the conversions on sales and traffic by channel. This can be done through setting up a goal monitor in Google Analytics. If you have set up multiple graphic ads on one channel then use your click thru data to track performance and make pivots.

Remember all channels should be echoing similar but different messages. Its best to not to take the same graphic ad and push it across multiple platforms, as you may cause brand fatigue.

Step 8: Recap

Just as important as creating an awesome holiday marketing campaign is your recap. Keep tabs on what performed well and what didn't. What you learn will help you make better decisions for next holiday. Your recap should be an excel document that lists each channel, graphic assets associated, conversion, traffic, sales by week and a written summary of each channel. Google Analytics will be able to provide you with a lot of the digital data, but your other marketing events and print media will have to be tracked manually.

Take the time to create this document. I know there are always a lot of things on your plate, but you will save a lot of money next season based on what you learn- trust me. Once you have taken the time to put it together, don't just shelf it never to be seen again. Revisit it again next season when you start planning for your next holiday!

PART TWO

Last Minute Strategy:
HOLIDAY PLANNING IN Q3/Q4

The holiday season is upon you! There is an opportunity for Q4 to be your biggest selling months yet. If you are new to creating marketing campaigns and sales planning for the holiday it can seem like a daunting task. You might be seeing other brands launching holiday collections or wondering how they staged their brand collaborations. Well, all these things take time. If you are looking to develop a cohesive holiday plan well in advance then take a look at the Getting a Head Start section. But, I am imaging you are reading this wondering what you can do today to impact your sales in the next 1-6 months. You are in luck- read on.

PRODUCTS

Assortment Planning

If you have the capacity to produce products quickly, then you have the ability to create holiday exclusives. These are products that you are going to market as holiday exclusives or as new deliveries to your retail partners. If you don't have the capacity to create newness in your assortment you may want to consider bundling a few items to create a new offering.

Your assortment should also be reflected in your online merchandising strategy. Make it easy for your customers to buy for their sister, mother, brother, husband or kids by adding new merchandising categories. Some examples to get inspired by: Top 5 Gifts for your Best Friend, Wow Gifts for Her, Favorites Under $50.

Markdowns and Pricing

Markdowns can be tough on your margins, especially when you haven't built them in to your pricing strategy. Most startup brands don't ever plan for the 20%-50% off you may need to take during the holiday season to get sell through. If you are in that boat, you may want to think about doing short-term sales – 3 or 4 days, instead of doing a hard markdown during the season. Advertising these little sales will help you drive traffic, and if you are listing on

Pinterest- it will really help. Did you know that every time you change your pricing on Pinterest it would automatically bump that post on the top for anyone who is following your brand? Its genius!

Pricing and Markdown example:
Your item costs $100 at retail, and $35 to make. That's a $65 margin and 2.85 markup. If you end up selling the item at $80, a 20% discount, it drops your margin to $45 and markup to 2.28. You may think your goal is to make as many sales as possible before reach the amount at cost. It is, kind of. In true essence your $65 margin is actually less. After you take into consideration your true costs of your business, how much you spend on operating costs, marketing and the rest, your real margin may be quite a bit less. So before you take deep price cuts to drive sales and traffic, keep in mind that your products are your lifelines and they need to maintain profitability to support your business. If you have the time to figure out or you actually know what your business margins are, then don't price down your products lower than that adjusted cost unless you are reacy to liquidate inventory and the new season is upon you.

MARKETING

Before starting anything, no matter how little time you have, its important to do your research and develop a plan. Before launching into the steps below its important to do a time assessment. What month is it? Is it November and you have $50 for marketing? Or is it November, you have $500 for marketing? Maybe it's August and you think you can wing it depending on what you think you need. No matter how much money you have to invest in your marketing strategy or what month it is lets make a plan.

Your plan will have a combination of your budget, timeframe, and goals.

Example: $500 marketing budget, 51 days (Nov 1st- Dec 21st), Sell prcduct. Then you can start to apply the strategies listed below and find the right combination to fit your needs. You will execute a combination of paid and unpaid marketing initiatives, but keep in mind its harder to develop organic brand partnerships and outside support if you don't have much time. If there is an idea you like and you don't have the time to execute on it, table it for next year.

Step 1: Research

Digital Marketing

You are no stranger at evaluating your own digital platforms. But have you analyzed it? Spend some time looking into your own platforms to see what people are engaging with. Make note of that content. Is there a core user base of followers on your platforms? These people will come in handy. The more organic your engagement the less your digital advertising spend needs are. If you are don't have much organic engagement then you will want to increase your budget for paid marketing and read on.

Facebook Ads:

I'm not a huge fan of Facebook for Facebook pages, but I do think their digital advertising is really smart. Leverage hyper targeting ad placements to get specific with who ends up seeing your ad. Remember: It's not about the number of people who come to your site, but the number of people who convert (a.k.a. buy things). Since you may not have a lot of time to test advertising to hone in on your Facebook target market, take an educated guess.

As you monitor and pivot your campaigns you may be able to make some tweaks based on what you find. For these ads you will be creating graphic assets to support it. If you need to hire someone fast to do it I suggest Upwork, TaskRabbit and 99designs. Make sure your ad lands on the right shop pages and that you have supporting banner ads to echo your messaging.

Example messages: Free 2 Day shipping Over $50, BOGO (buy one get one free), Free Shipping with Code HOL15.

Cost to Create: I suggest starting Facebook ads around $50 for

10 days.

Time Needed to Setup: 1 hour (including graphics and ad set up)

Twitter Ads:

Twitter has updated their advertising platform to allow for more dynamic product advertising. If you have an active Twitter account then this is a good option for you. If you don't then I wouldn't suggest hopping on Twitter right away just to do these ads. The cool thing about Twitter ads is that they allow you to target your competitor's handles directly. This will allow you to market to your competitor's audience. If this is a good fit for you, you will need to reformat and change your ad specs to accommodate this platform.

Cost to Create: Graphic design + Ad cost: $100-$200 for 15 days.
Time Needed to Setup: 1 hour

Pinterest:

This is a good platform to use for selling. If you have been on this platform for a while I do suggest taking advantage of dynamic pins. At this moment Pinterest is getting ready to open up promoted pins, so you will have to join the waitlist to be notified when it opens up. When you do engage with dynamic pins and change pricing on your products it will bubble to the top of the feed for your followers.

Tip: Do price changes just for the weekend to get the visibility.

Cost to Create: $0 – Cost of Graphic Designer / Photographer
Time Needed to Setup: To make sure your pins are all dynamic it might take some time, depending on how many you have 1-3 hours.

Instagram:

Until they open up their platform to allow smaller brands to engage in advertising this will remain and organic channel for our purposes. The best way to leverage your organic audience will be through giveaways that generate likes, reposts and tagging.

If you have some time to do research into influencer marketing you may be able to get on the radar of high ranking influencers, but be cautious of high ranking influencers who don't have much engagement on their platforms. Its too easy to buy followers these days, so if you get awed by an influencers 45k followers see if they have a 5% conversion rate (2,250 likes). To track your sales generated by Instagram use Google short links and alternate the products promoted on your channels by day.

Cost to Create: To work with influencers expect to pay between $10-$1,000
Time Needed to Setup: As quickly as you can edit images!

YouTube:

Does your brand have a YouTube channel? Have you thought about partnering with a v-logger (video blogger)? If you have a YouTube channel, you may want to create a short promo video about the holiday season. Maybe it's a sneak peak into the office and talks about your best selling holiday products. Maybe you are offering ideas on what to give for the holiday. These can be free to produce and be edited very fast. On YouTube make sure you connect the links to your product pages! If you couple this will an ad spend it could become a place to drive sales for your brand.

Cost to Create: Free + Cost of Ad: $100-$500
Time Needed to Setup: Give yourself 2 weeks to make sure editing is done well.

Banner Ads:

Creating a banner ad on your site is a great way to harness your own traffic to convert. Keep your messaging consistent, especially if you have different ad promos running. Purchasing banner advertising on niche market websites is also a great option. Smaller, more targeted publications will also be speaking directly to your customer and they wont be targeted by larger brands- so do some digging you might find some jewels.

Cost to Create: Graphic designer + Placement: $100-$750
Time Needed to Setup: Since you are relying on the availability of these spaces, the earlier you start the better. 1-3 months.

Dedicated Blog Posts/Dedicated Newsletters/:

Similar to the Banner Ads, if you are looking for placement on another parties channel it takes a little time. Do some research into niche markets and find potential partners that your product will make a great fit for. It should be a natural fit, as if there audience were to say "but of course this product/brand would go in my closet/shelf". If you do find a great opportunity make sure that you find out the number of people your placement will reach, and what similar advertisements have converted.

Cost to Create: Graphic Assets + Post ($100-2,000)
Time Needed to Setup: The more time the better! At least 1 month.

Direct Marketing

Getting in front of your customer has to take on a 360° approach. It's not enough to rely on digital to get the word out. It does take time to create direct marketing assets, find the right outlets, negotiate pricing and get placed. Long-lead publications take 3 months and smaller ones take about 1 month. Keep in mind that the holiday season is the biggest time for ad spending, next to the Super Bowl. The earlier you plan this- the better. While your timing and budget may be limited there are a few things you can do to generate sales.

Popup Shops:

Putting together a multi-brand pop up shop can happen very quickly if you already know who you want to work with. Think about the brands that currently target your same demographic but are selling different kinds of products. Make sure your pricing is aligned, doesn't make sense to have a luxury brand trying to sell to an entry-level price brand. Check out resources like thestorefront.com to get a read on what spaces are available in your target area. You will need to make sure you have inventory to sell and to make it a cohesive campaign will want to have postcards, stickers for shopping bags and back it all up with some placement on your digital channels.

Cost to Create: Depending on how extensive: $700-$5,000
Time Needed to Setup: 3-12 weeks

Postcards:

Having postcards handy are great for passing out at events, leaving at local coffee shops, mailing out to your existing customer base and to your trusty list of bloggers and editors. Use a beautiful image of your product and include your all relevant contact details plus a few key words or sentences about your brand. To get extra oomph out of it have small stickers printed up with a few targeted coupon codes. You can stick them on before an event or marketing opportunity to track effectiveness of bounce back to your site.

Cost to Create: $100 + Postage
Time Needed to Setup: 2-3 hours

Print Advertising: Magazines, Newspapers, and Periodicals:

For a last minute strategy this type of outlet can be the toughest to target. I only suggest using these channels as a supporting campaign to your digital or live events. Its tough to track the conversions on these ads, and even with bounce back codes the conversions can be quite low. Heads up: most print advertising will have longer lead times for deadlines. If you are running out of time but want to include this type of channel then look to weekly publications since they might still have some openings.

Cost to Create: Graphic Designer + Placement: $200-$1500
Time Needed to Setup: 1-3 months

Step 2: Outreach

Since you are on a short timeline you need to find out quickly which paid and unpaid channels you are going to go forward with. Start by outreaching to the paid channels first to get an idea of deadlines and cost. Make sure to get all relevant data on the target market, reach numbers, and what assets you will need to create the best campaign ever.

Example Email:

Hi Cristina!

I hope you are great. I'd like to chat with you about November/December ad placement on Man Repeller. Could you let me know what your deadlines are for submission and your ad rates? Right now I am looking into <insert type of ads>.

Thanks!
Syama

Step 3: Budget

Now while we would love to do everything on our list of potential outreach, we need to optimize for budget and timing. Normally I would suggest we create the budget based on your overall marketing budget for the year, but if this is last minute here is what I suggest. Set aside a minimum of $5 a day on your digital marketing campaigns until you get some solid data on what is working. This should be evident after 7 days of advertising. Once you get a sense of your responsive target market then up your budget and keep trekking.

Creating graphic assets, while echoed throughout this guide, is often overlooked. This aspect can take time and you want to make sure you have the right dimensions and call-to-actions in place. If you aren't creating these yourself then look to some outside help. A copywriter might also be in your budget if you aren't the strongest writer. A general rule of thumb your annual marketing budget should be about 15% of your yearly sales. This very much applies to businesses that have tested and gained target insight. In your first 12 months of business expect to amp up your spend between $1200-$5000.

Step 4: Develop Timeline

No matter how little or much time you have a timeline is important. Create an excel spreadsheet with the platforms both paid and unpaid and track it out by week. What channels launch when and what assets need to be finalized by when. Also track your goals and expectations. Are you targeting a niche market? You might have a small out reach but a higher expectation on click thru's and conversions.

Tip on conversion: make sure you have a newsletter pop up ready on your site to capture all these new leads!

Step 5: Develop Assets

Get creative! If you don't have Photoshop then I suggest using simple graphic design programs like Canva and PicMonkey. Make sure your graphic assets are cohesive, with the same branded fonts and design direction. For this reason its best to either have a style guide for consistency purposes or to have the same designer create all your assets and then create the style guide afterwards. Be clear on the dimensions you need and what content can be put on the graphics or on the text portion of your post. Many ads allow you to create multiple variations to test you image and text, so be sure to take advantage of this.

Step 6: Launch

Whoohoo! You made it. The work is almost over. Remember to be patient and to keep in mind that marketing is a long tail game. The first time you see an ad will you buy it right it away? You might buy it, but you also might not. In many cases it takes up to 3 different social proofs before a potential client converts, hence why I push the multi pronged approach.

Step 7: Monitor & Pivot

Even if your campaign is only 7 days long its important to track data on performance. Use your timeline and goal sheet and add your results right next to it. If your campaign is longer then monitor which ads are performing best and redirect your ad dollars to those ads. Having multiple styles of ads will allow you to compare more effectively. Maybe it's the image with the model that's getting the most traffic, maybe it's the clear product shot. Creating the tests to get the answers to need.

Step 8: Recap

A post-mortem allows you to recap what worked and didn't work during your campaign. Remember the whole point of doing all of this is to make sales! Over time you will develop the channels that work for your brand but you need to keep records so that next year when you start to plan for Holiday again you can improve your odds of conversions.

Tip: Add a reminder on your calendar for February of the following year to review your recap and start to think about holiday again.

PRINT & POST

Print and post these tips where you can see it.

A Cohesive Campaign is:

- Digital and Direct
- Supported on all your platforms
- Tracked with Google Analytics and custom campaign url's
- Visually well designed
- Set up with goals and metrics
- Set up with a timeline
- Set up with a budget

Your Checklist for Success:

- Analyze & Research potential and current channels
- Develop Budget
- Develop Timeline
- Develop Assets
- Launch!
- Monitor & Pivot
- Recap

5-day Social Media Posting Tip:
Stagger your messaging

Day 1: Post goes up on your blog or Newsletter
Day 2: Post goes up on Instagram
Day 3: Post goes up on Facebook
Day 4: Post goes up on Pinterest
Day 5: Post goes up on Twitter

PARTING WORDS...

Congratulations! Its time to get started on everything you have learned.

No matter what time of the year it is it's never too late to start thinking about your holiday sales strategy. I like to stress advanced planning because it really gives you the benefit of cultivating relationships and maximizing your advertising spend. But if you are doing this last minute there are a lot of ways to make an impact, delve deeper into understanding your customer and make holiday sales.

Keep me posted on your progress and let me know if you have any questions.

All my best,
Syama

CEO, Scaling Retail
www.ScalingRetail.com

Lightning Source UK Ltd.
Milton Keynes UK
UKHW012031051121
393447UK00001B/88